AF300833

Lothar-Rüdiger Lütge

The Veneration of the
Blessed Virgin Mary

**A guide to understanding the
Mother of God for reformed Christians and
people of other faiths.**

FSC
www.fsc.org
MIX
Papier aus ver-
antwortungsvollen
Quellen
Paper from
responsible sources
FSC® C105338

Production and publishing:
BoD – Books on Demand,
Norderstedt, Germany

ISBN: 9 783757 830595

The Veneration of the Blessed Virgin Mary

A guide to understanding the Mother of God for reformed Christians and people of other faiths.

The veneration that Catholic and Orthodox Christians bring to the Blessed Virgin Mary often encounters misunderstanding and confusion outside these traditional churches. In particular, reformed Christians of various denominations often struggle to comprehend the intense devotion and appreciation with which Catholics and Orthodox approach the Mother of God.

The Catholic Church refers to Mary as the Queen of Heaven, or also the Queen of Angels. It sees in Mary a truly special, outstanding human being. According to the teachings of the church, Mary, after Adam and Eve, is the third human being created by God without original sin. She is something like a new Eve. Thus, she holds a completely extraordinary position in humanity.

So, Mary is not just a particularly devout young woman who, two thousand years ago in Palestine, willingly submitted to God's will, became pregnant by the Holy Spirit, and gave birth to Jesus after nine months. Mary herself was already conceived without original sin by her mother Anna. So even before her own birth, when Mary was conceived, God ensured that original sin did not pass onto her. Thus, God prepared the birth of his son Jesus through the Virgin Mary already at her conception. When Mary was conceived by her parents, Joachim and Anna, God broke the chain of original sin for Mary. Why did God do this? Because His son, Jesus Christ, of course, cannot enter the world through a sinful human. Jesus Christ is fully human and fully God. And where God is, there can be no sin. For the incarnation, God needed a pure vessel, a pure human, a pure virgin who voluntarily agreed to receive God's son and bring him into the world.

Even this understanding of the Blessed Virgin Mary goes far beyond all assumptions and statements made by the reformed churches regarding Mary. But the details we have considered so far, which only refer to the Immaculate Conception of Mary, are just the tip of the iceberg. To fully understand the traditional significance of the Mother of God, we must consider the differences in the world view and human image between the ancient Christian tradition and the reformed Christian churches. This is particularly relevant as Mary, along with Jesus Christ himself, is at the center of veneration for many Catholic and Orthodox Christians.

Let's first look at the images of humanity. According to traditional Christian teaching, a human being consists of the body as well as the soul or spirit. In traditional Christian teaching, the terms soul and spirit are often used synonymously, and sometimes the combined term 'spirit-soul' is used. While the body arises at the biological level in the act of procreation and then grows in the mother's womb, the soul or spirit is created by God parallel to conception. The body is material and subject to physical laws, the soul is spiritual and it exists beyond space and time, i.e. it exists forever after God has created it. Thus, a human being is an eternal spiritual being that temporarily possesses a material body. In these aspects, Catholicism, Orthodoxy, and the Reformed churches largely agree. However, there are also important differences.

Traditional Christian teaching assumes that when a person dies, body and soul are separated. The body becomes non-functional with physical death and decays, but the soul is immortal, it continues to live, in the hereafter, that is, in the spiritual world. There, it has three realms available: heaven, purgatory, and hell. Depending on its personal state, which results from the sum of its actions and omissions during its earthly life, and above all, depending on the grace of God, the soul enters one of these three realms. The souls of people who have fully complied with divine requirements during their life and are completely in a state of grace enter heaven. The souls that deliberately and intentionally violated the divine commandments to a massive extent and reject a final turn to God and His grace, enter hell. And the souls who have not fully complied with God's commands, but have striven to do so, and whose individual guilt is not final, enter purgatory. There they can undergo purification, with the aim, later, after successful purgation, to still experience God's grace in full and thus enter heaven. According to this original Christian view, life in heaven, purgatory, and hell extends until the Last Judgment on the Last Day. Then, God creates a new heaven and a new earth. This is a greatly simplified representation of traditional Christian ideas about the life and death of humans, as fundamentally taught in the Roman Catholic and Orthodox Church to this day.

Against all these notions, however, Martin Luther opposed. He denied that the human spirit-soul continues to live uninterruptedly in the afterlife after death. As he based his views exclusively on his personal interpretation of biblical texts and rejected the original teachings and traditions of the Church, he also rejected the church doctrine of the afterlife. According to his understanding, he found no written evidence for it in the Bible. In his opinion, the human soul falls into a kind of sleep state without consciousness at the death of the human being, i.e., at the separation of body and spirit, in which it remains permanently and in this unconscious state waits for God to awaken it on the Last Day and reunite it with its then newly created body. So, in Lutheran faith, there is no conscious life after death and no living souls in the afterlife, but only an unconscious existence and the bodily-spiritual resurrection promised by God on the Last Day. This distinction between the traditional, Christian and the reformed, Lutheran human image is very important, as it results in very different worldviews.

While in the worldview of Catholics and Orthodox Christians, the otherworldly, spiritual world is not only populated by many angels and demons but also by the countless souls of the deceased, which move in various realms and interact in diverse ways with each other, the afterlife for Luther and the reformed churches he initiated is completely devoid of humans. Although the existence of angels and demons as spiritual beings is fundamentally acknowledged, the existence of conscious, otherworldly human souls is not recognized. This is one of the profound theological differences that led to the Reformation and Luther's break with the Catholic Church. The so-called indulgence trade was just the trigger of the dispute. This practice was particularly thorny to Luther because, in his opinion, there is neither an otherworldly world with living human souls nor a purgatory. In Luther's view, the faithful were thus deceived by the church.

From a traditional Christian perspective, however, the situation is completely different and it is very important for a deeper understanding of the veneration of Mary to understand the mutual influence of people in the material world on the souls in the spiritual world, and vice versa. Therefore, it may be helpful to take a closer look at what the so-called indulgence in the Catholic Church is really about. The necessary premise here is the traditional Christian worldview: After that, there is an otherworldly world and there are spiritual beings and the souls of the deceased. Many of these souls will, to human estimation, likely be in purgatory, undergoing the purification and purgation necessary for the kingdom of heaven. And now it is part of traditional Christian knowledge that as a person still living on earth, one can intercede with God for these souls in purgatory. This means that one can ask God, for example, to be merciful to a deceased person and to shorten their purgation in purgatory. And one can further support this petition to God by oneself, in place of the deceased, making a sacrifice for them, such as donating a sum of money for good purposes, in the name of the deceased. So one voluntarily gives up a part of what one has earned for oneself, as a sacrifice to God - or vicariously to other people - to give weight to one's own petition to God. This is the principle underlying indulgence. The indulgence system only makes sense if one understands and accepts these premises.

Conversely, according to traditional Christian belief, a saint in heaven, an angel, a deceased person (or their soul), and particularly the Virgin Mary, can intercede with God on behalf of a living person and thereby bring about good for them. The system, therefore, works reciprocally! The spiritual world and the material world are interconnected by a kind of permeable membrane. Worldly and heavenly events can influence each other and do so. This becomes evident, among other things, by the fact that, according to traditional Christian teaching, many angels and saints attend the celebration of each Holy Mass. While invisible to living people, they are nonetheless spiritually present. Furthermore, the Catholic and Orthodox Churches attribute immediate spiritual effects to the celebration of every Holy Mass. The same applies to the sacraments of the Catholic Church. Here too, the material action brings about a concrete spiritual effect. And conversely, devout Christians who turn to the holy Virgin Mary for help, or consciously place themselves under her protection, report that they experience concrete help in the material world.

Martin Luther and the reformed churches he initiated largely reject all these premises. For Luther and his successors, there is no immediate survival of individual souls after death in heaven, hell, or purgatory. Instead, the reformed churches teach a resurrection of the dead on the Last Day. Therefore, the idea that we as living people can intervene with God on behalf of the dead, or that conversely, the dead can intercede with God for us, seems utterly absurd to Luther and his successors.

In contrast, interaction and communication with the inhabitants of the spiritual world are an essential part of the religion for Catholic and Orthodox Christians. Catholics and Orthodox regularly invoke the intercession of certain canonized individuals whom they venerate as saints. These are people who led a particularly pleasing life to God during their lifetime and who are believed to now be in the kingdom of heaven with God as human souls after their earthly death. These holy souls thus have direct access to God and can intercede with Him for us and our concerns. The Catholic Church recognizes hundreds of these holy souls in the afterlife and recommends that believers turn to them in prayer in order to gain support from God for their own concerns through them.

Only with knowledge of this theological background does the veneration of the Virgin Mary and the turn towards her become understandable for reformed Christians and people of other faiths. Mary, who is in the unique position of being both virgin and mother of Jesus, is regarded in the Catholic and Orthodox tradition with a veneration that surpasses any other saint's veneration. She embodies pure purity, without any stain. She is as mankind should be, as it was thought and created by God, before it was tempted by Satan to turn away from its creator. And this holy Virgin Mary, after leaving the earth, is in heaven, with her son Jesus Christ, with God, and with the Holy Spirit. And from there she can and will intercede for us. She advocates for each individual who consciously turns to her and actively asks her, as well as for humanity in general. Mary acts as an intercessor for people before God and has revealed her care and help in numerous appearances over the centuries, until the recent past, all over the world.

The Catholic Church sees Mary as the spiritual mother of all Christians and as the mother of the Church. She gave her the titles "Queen of Heaven" and "Queen of Angels". So her status of sanctity is rated higher than that of the angels. She ranks in the heavenly hierarchy directly below the divine Trinity of Father, Son, and Holy Spirit. Contrary to the frequently heard accusations of reformed Christians, Mary is by no means "deified" in the realm of Catholic and Orthodox faith. And she is not equated with God either. She is seen as a particularly revered saint, who due to her unique role as the mother of Jesus and her closeness to God holds a special position in heaven. Mary advocates for the human race, which she herself comes from, and as its most exalted representative she acts.

According to traditional Christian conception, Mary plays a special role in God's plan for the world, especially in relation to the redemption of humanity through Jesus Christ. As the "second Eve", through her willingness to become pregnant by the Holy Spirit and give birth to the divine Son Jesus Christ, she made up for the mistake of the first Eve - our common ancestress, who let herself be seduced by the devil in Paradise. Her son, Jesus

Christ, the Son of God, is to crush the serpent, i.e., the fallen angel Lucifer, the adversary of God. Some traditions even see Mary herself as the one who ultimately carries out Satan's destruction. This is reported in the Bible from the very beginning, in the Book of Genesis, Chapter 3.

Thus, in Catholicism and Orthodoxy, Mary is regarded as a very special woman, or more generally, a very special person. In Catholic theology, Mary is considered unique among humans, as she was born without the stain of original sin according to the doctrine of the Immaculate Conception. Because of her purity and her spotless life, Mary, after her time on earth, was directly taken up to heaven, body and soul, according to Catholic and some Orthodox doctrines by God. The physical assumption into heaven was possible because Mary was without original sin and therefore not subject to death. In the heavenly hereafter, she lives in close proximity to God, to her son Jesus Christ, and to the Holy Spirit, and she advocates for people! As the Queen of Heaven and Mother of the Church and Christendom, she asks God for grace and help for humans.

In addition to Mary, there are many other saints who live in heaven close to God, as well as a vast number of angels who are devoted to God, worship Him and fulfill His will. All these instances are available to devout Catholics and Orthodox for invocation. Mary, the angels, and the saints can always be reached through our prayers, and they are ready and willing to intercede for us with God if we sincerely and with a pure heart ask them to.

In summary, in the Catholic tradition, there are four church doctrines, called dogmas, that define the properties and status of Mary:

1. The Divine Motherhood of Mary: Mary is the mother of Jesus Christ and thus also the mother of God.

2. The Virgin Birth: Mary conceived Jesus through the Holy Spirit and thus remained a virgin forever despite her pregnancy.

3. The Immaculate Conception: Mary herself was conceived and born without original sin.

4. The Assumption of Mary into Heaven: After her death, Mary was assumed into heaven body and soul.

These doctrines apply within the Catholic Church and, with variations, also in Orthodox Christianity.

The devotion of believers to the Mother of God takes place in a ceremonial form, in special church Marian devotions and prayer times. The Catholic Church long ago designated the month of May specifically as the "Month of Mary," and regular Marian devotions take place in the churches. On the other hand, the daily personal prayer to the Mother of God is the central and most important way for a Catholic Christian to connect with Mary and express his deep connection with her.

There are many widespread and less known Marian prayers. The "Hail Mary" is the most famous and essential of all Marian prayers. The text of the Hail Mary consists of two parts, which originated in different historical contexts. The first part of the prayer comes directly from the Bible and includes the words addressed to Mary by the Archangel Gabriel and Elizabeth, the mother of John the Baptist. These statements are found in the Gospel of Luke (Luke 1:28 and Luke 1:42):

"Hail Mary, full of grace, the Lord is with thee." (Lk 1:28)
"Blessed art thou among women, and blessed is the fruit of thy womb, Jesus." (Lk 1:42)

The second part of the prayer, which asks Mary for her intercession, was added later and has taken various forms over the centuries. The current wording:

"Holy Mary, Mother of God, pray for us sinners, now and at the hour of our death. Amen."

was established during the Council of Trent (1545-1563) in the 16th century.

Put together, the Hail Mary reads:

Hail Mary, full of grace, the Lord is with thee. Blessed art thou among women and blessed is the fruit of thy womb, Jesus. Holy Mary, Mother of God, pray for us sinners, now and at the hour of our death. Amen.

The Hail Mary is one of the most frequently spoken prayers in Catholic Christianity. It is used in different contexts, especially in personal prayer and particularly in the Rosary prayer. The Rosary is a meditative form of prayer in which the Hail Mary, alternating with other prayers and with specific statements about the stations in the life and death of Jesus, is repeated 53 times in total. Catholic Christians pray the Rosary either alone or in groups, where they then alternate from verse to verse.

Another widely used prayer to the Virgin Mary is the "Sub Tuum Praesidium". This is the oldest known and still used Marian prayer. The oldest existing records of this prayer are written in Greek and date from the 3rd century:

"We fly to thy protection, O Holy Mother of God, Despise not our petitions in our necessities, But deliver us always from all dangers. O Glorious and Blessed Virgin "

A frequently added second part of the prayer comes from a later time:

"Our Lady, our Mediator, our Advocate. Reconcile us to your Son, Recommend us to your Son, present us before your Son."

So, put together, the prayer reads:

We fly to thy protection, O Holy Mother of God, Despise not our petitions in our necessities, But deliver us always from all dangers. O Glorious and Blessed Virgin.

Our Lady, our Mediator, our Advocate. Reconcile us to your Son, Recommend us to your Son, present us before your Son.

Finally, a short prayer to Mary should be mentioned, which the Holy Virgin herself gave us during her apparitions in 1830 in Paris. At that time, the Virgin Mary repeatedly appeared to the nun Catherine Labouré and asked her to have a protective medal made for people in need. The medal should have, among other details, the following inscription:

O Mary, conceived without sin, pray for us who have recourse to thee.

The medal quickly spread widely in the Catholic world. In the very first years, several million copies were made and distributed. It is now distributed worldwide and is still worn by many Catholics around the world. Due to the frequent reports of very concrete help that believers have received from the Mother of God, this medal is known as the "Miraculous Medal". It is of course clear to devout Catholics that the medal itself does not perform miracles and that the role of the Holy Virgin Mary is that of a mediator. Mary intercedes for us with her Son Jesus Christ, God the Father, and the Holy Spirit. Her role is that of an advocate. Maria, Mediatrix of Graces (Latin: Maria Mediatrix) is an attribute or invocation of Mary, the mother of Jesus, used in the Roman Catholic Church. Mary serves as a mediator of grace, which we receive from God.

In conclusion, it should be noted that the above explanations are intended solely to provide a general understanding of the traditional veneration of the Holy Virgin Mary for reformed Christians and believers of other faiths. In order to achieve the clearest and most meaningful representation possible, the theological contents and teachings of the individual denominations and faith directions have been simplified to some extent. Furthermore, in favor of general clarity and overview, a detailed differentiation in detail was omitted. At the same time, efforts were made to avoid gross inaccuracies or false attributions. The intentions underlying the explanations are exclusively constructive and positive. Should believers of any Christian denomination or other faith direction recognize deficiencies in the representation of faith convictions, indulgence is requested.